# CREATE, COOK AND CONQUER
## 15 EASY DELICIOUS BARIATRIC RECIPES TO KEEP THE WEIGHT OFF!

©Author: Chef Cynthia Monden

# ©Text Copyright 2020 by Chef Cynthia Monden

All rights reserved. No part of this guide may be reproduced in any form without permission in writing from the publisher except in the case of brief quotations embodied in critical articles or reviews.

---

## Legal & Disclaimer

The content and information contained in this book has been compiled from sources deemed reliable, and it is accurate to the best of the Author's knowledge, information and belief. However, the Author cannot guarantee its accuracy and validity and cannot be held liable for any errors and/or omissions. Further, changes are periodically made to this book as and when needed. Where appropriate and/or necessary, you must consult a professional (including but not limited to your doctor, attorney, financial advisor or such other professional advisor) before using any of the suggested remedies, techniques, or information in this book.

Upon using the contents and information contained in this book, you agree to hold harmless the Author from and against any damages, costs, and expenses, including any legal fees potentially resulting from the application of any of the information provided by this book.

## About the Author, "Chef Cynthia Monden"

In September 2017, I decided to take a bold step towards changing my life. I loved food since I was a little girl. Food was my comfort. I ate anytime I was happy, sad, hungry, overjoyed, or even depressed. But unfortunately, the food I ate was full of junk and was literally killing me. I was seriously obese, weighing around 299 pounds. I couldn't bear to look at myself, gather around friends or even go to the party anymore. I wonder how I got "here"! After a candid conversation with my doctor and my husband, we decided that the Vertical Sleeve Gastrectomy (VSG surgery) would be the best for my unwarranted condition. I didn't have any diseases but I was extremely overweight. During the course of 10 months, I lost about 35 pounds before the surgery. On July 18, 2018, I went under the knife and it completely changes my life. I mean, I literally begin to see amazing body transformations. Things change right away. I couldn't eat, barely anything, but protein shakes and drink water. I had to drink at least 64 oz of water a day. The food I did eat was bland and didn't agree with my new tummy. After achieving great success, I now feel inspired to create this amazingly flavorful recipe cookbook to share my kitchen and culinary experience especially to people like me trying to lose weight.

# My Image Before Weight Loss

# My Image During VSG Surgery...

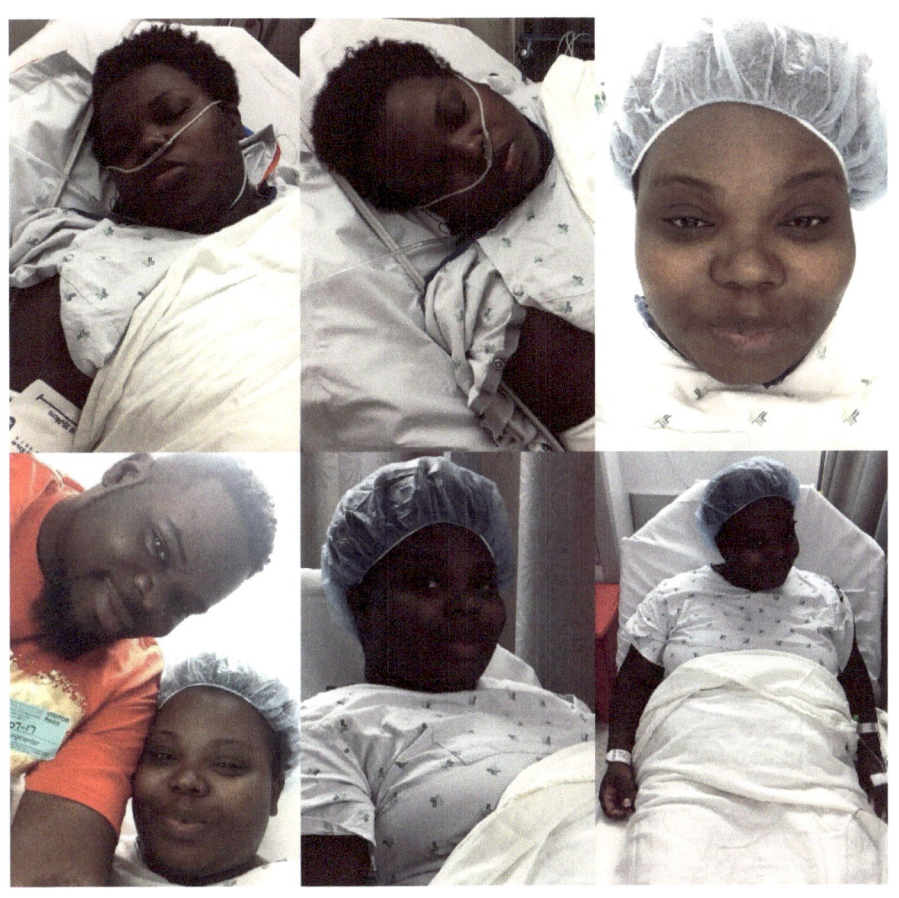

# Before And After Weight Loss

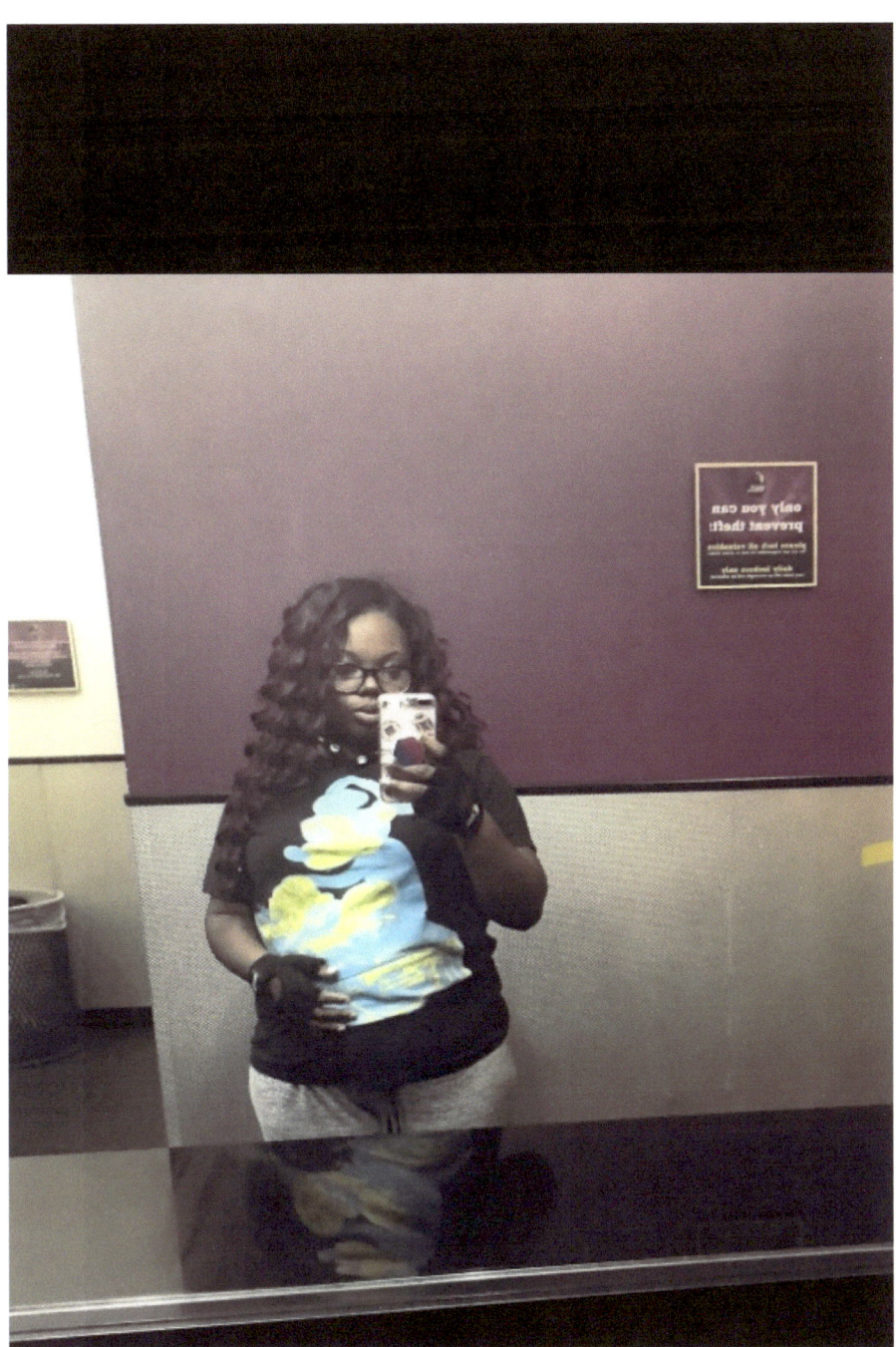

# TABLE OF CONTENTS

**Introduction** ..................................................................................11
**15 Done For You Awesome Bariatrics Recipes!** ...............13
    **Cheese Cake Pudding** ........................................................13
    **Pumpkin Pie Spice Coffee** ................................................15
    **Caramel protein shake** .....................................................17
    **White chocolate protein shake** ......................................19
    **Lemon ricotta crème** ........................................................21
    **Guacamole Bowl** ................................................................23
    **Spicy Roasted Chicken w/ Mashed potato and lemon peas** ..........................................................................26
    **Mashed Potato** ...................................................................28
    **Lemon Peas** ........................................................................31
    **Frozen Caramel Coffee** ....................................................33
    **Raspberry delight** .............................................................35
    **Colorful Tuna** .....................................................................37
    **Energy Bites** ......................................................................39
    **Zucchini Noodles with Chicken Breast** .......................41
    **Creamy Cajun Shrimp Pasta** ..........................................43
**Conclusion** ..................................................................................46

# Introduction

If you are suffering from severe obesity, getting a sleeve gastrectomy procedure just might be the answer for you. Also known as vertical gastrectomy, this type of procedure is a restrictive weight loss surgery, which reduces the size of the stomach. Although this surgical treatment is irreversible, vertical gastrectomy is fast providing a growing number of obese patients with life-saving benefits.

Vertical Sleeve Gastrectomy is a rare type of restrictive bariatric obesity surgery. Until now, it is performed by a limited number of surgeons worldwide. The original procedure was known as The Magenstrasse and Mill Operation which allows rapid weight loss by restricting the amount of food intake with mal-absorption or bypass of the intestines. The size of the stomach pouch is smaller than the pouch used in the Duodenal Switch.

Safe for patients with high-risk and high Body Mass Index (BMI), this surgical treatment is able to remove up to 85% of the stomach, and allows you to lose 100 pounds or more. By getting a vertical gastrectomy, you'll be able to reduce or perhaps even completely eliminate medical issues that result from obesity. These include diabetes, high cholesterol, heart disease, as well as lack of mobility and quality of life.

After bariatric surgery, your meal portions are much smaller. Your new diet helps you progress with weight loss in a nutritionally sound manner to reach your health goals. Eating a variety of foods will help you obtain adequate protein, vitamins and minerals. To help increase the variety in your diet, the Bariatric Surgery Program is offering a selection of recipes for you to enjoy.

As you continue to lose weight, it is important to develop and maintain healthy eating habits. Success with weight loss will depend on your adherence to nutritious food choices and avoiding snacking or "grazing" between meals. The stomach pouch created by your surgery is a tool you will need to become accustomed to in order to meet your weight loss goals.

# 15 Done For You Awesome Bariatrics Recipes!

## Cheese Cake Pudding

This simple, yet slightly indulgent recipe is one you'll want to make again and again. You can serve in pretty parfait glasses or use mason jars for a more casual setting.

**Total Time: 5**

**Servings: 1**

## Ingredients

1 cup plain fat-free Greek yogurt

1 package sugar-free cheesecake pudding mix

## Directions

1. Combine all ingredients in a blender and puree until smooth.

# Pumpkin Pie Spice Coffee

Simple three ingredient recipe for making pumpkin pie spice coffee at home. Zero calories and bariatric friendly!

**Total Time: 5 min**

**Servings: 4**

| Ingredients | Directions |
|---|---|
| 6 tbsp Ground Coffee<br><br>1/4 tsp Pumpkin Pie Spice<br><br>4 cups water | 1. Add coffee grounds to coffee maker and add pumpkin pie spice to the grounds. Use a spoon to lightly stir in the spice.<br>2. Brew coffee as you usually do! |

# Caramel protein shake

This bariatric friendly shake is a classic vanilla shake with added flavors from caramel and almond extract. Having this shake in the evening instead of a sweet treat is also a great idea.

**Total Time: 5 min**

**Servings: 1**

## Ingredients

- 1/4 cup low-fat cottage cheese
- 1 scoop whey vanilla protein powder
- 1/2 tsp caramel extract
- 1/2 tsp almond extract
- 1 cup water
- 6 ice cubes

## Directions

1. Combine all ingredients in a blender and blend on high until smooth.

# White chocolate protein shake

This bariatric friendly shake is certainly on the sweet side. It's so delicious and healthy way to start your morning, pre-workout, or to just get a boost throughout the day!

**Total Time: 5 mint**

**Servings: 1**

| Ingredients | Directions |
|---|---|
| 8 ounces unsweetened almond milk<br><br>6 ice cubes<br><br>1 scoop vanilla whey protein powder<br><br>1/2 tbsp sugar free white chocolate pudding mix | 1. Add all the ingredients to a blender and blend on high until smooth. |

# Lemon ricotta crème

This delicious recipe is based on a healthy balance between carbohydrates and fats. The purpose of the diet is to change the balance of foods you eat and encourage healthy food choices, which will lead to weight loss.

**Total Time: 5**

**Servings: 1**

| Ingredients | Directions |
|---|---|
| 15 oz. container of low-fat/fat-free ricotta cheese<br><br>zest of one lemon (or orange)<br><br>1-2 tsp. lemon extract (or orange extract)<br><br>1 1/2 teaspoons of vanilla extract<br><br>4 packets of Splenda | 1. Place all ingredients in a blender and puree until smooth. |

# Guacamole Bowl

If you want to make the best guacamole, just keep it simple:- ripe avocados, salt, a squeeze of lime, onions, chiles, cilantro, and some chopped tomato. Serve it as a dip at your next party or spoon it on top of tacos for an easy dinner upgrade.

**Total Time: 10 min**

**Servings: 4**

## Ingredients

4 Ripe Avocado pitted

½ pound of ground turkey

¼ cup of small diced tomatoes

¼ cup red onions

½ cup of cilantro

1 jalapeno

1/3 cup white cheddar

¼ cup of olive oil

a pinch of salt

1 tablespoon of white pepper

1 tbsp of paprika

2 tbsp of garlic

## Directions

1. In a medium bowl mash together the avocado, lime juice, lemon juice and salt. Fold in the red onion, tomato, cilantro, jalapeno
2. In a skittle add olive oil, ground turkey cook to 165 degree and add white pepper, garlic powder, paprika, salt, and onion powder.
3. Fill the cavity of the avocado with the ground turkey and add the guacamole on top with the white cheddar.

powder

3 tbsp of onion powder

1 lemon

1 lime

## Spicy Roasted Chicken w/ Mashed potato and lemon peas

With a recipe that includes chicken breasts, you're just minutes away from the most addictive Garlic Chicken dinner the whole family loves! The perfect meal to have when you feel like eating something sweet with a hint of savoury.

**Total Time: 25 min**

**Servings: 1**

| Ingredients | Directions |
|---|---|
| 1 pound of chicken breast<br><br>Olive oil<br><br>1Salt<br><br>Black pepper<br><br>Red Pepper flakes<br><br>Onion powder<br><br>Garlic powder<br><br>Smoked Paprika<br><br>Lemon pepper<br><br>Chicken broth | 1. Pre heated the oven at 325 degree. Mix all the season together Col the chicken breast with olive oil then sprinkle the season on top of the breast.<br>2. Place the chicken in a deep dish pan add chicken broth at the bottom. Roasted the chicken breast for 30 to 35 minute. |

# Mashed Potato

Mashed Potatoes are super simple to make with very few ingredients. You can make them in the Crock Pot or Instant Pot, but I really do think the best mashed potatoes are a simple classic. Simple and delicious!

**Total Time: 25 – 30 min**

**Servings: 2**

## Ingredients

1 pound Yukon Gold potatoes

½ pound Parsnips

3 T Unsalted butter

¼ c Heavy cream

½ tsp Sea salt

1T White pepper

Parsley

## Directions

1. Peel the potato and parsnip and cut them into even chunks. Place them in a pot of COLD water. Add the salt and turn on to the high heat until the water come to a boil.
2. Boil the potato and parsnip for about 10-12 minutes or until it fork tender.
3. Carefully drain out the water.
4. Meanwhile as the potato and parsnip is boiling, heat up you unsalted butter, heavy cream and sea salt.
5. In the pot mashed the potato and parsnip to your desired consistency then fold the heavy cream mixer to the potato and parsnip.
6. Add white pepper, sea salt and parsley to your taste. Serve warm

# Lemon Peas

This peas recipe takes just 5 minutes! Cooking frozen peas with zest lemon makes them taste incredible. It's an easy side dish everyone will love!

**Total Time: 7 min**

**Servings: 1**

## Ingredients

1 bag of frozen green peas

1 T Unsalted butter

1 lemon

Lemon zest

¼ c Chicken broth

Pinch of pink Salt

## Directions

1. Place green peas into a small pot and sauté with chicken broth, lemon juice and zest, pink salt and unsalted butter for 5 to 7 minute then serve.

# Frozen Caramel Coffee

Frozen Caramel Coffee is a smooth frozen blended drink, it's rich, buttery and fabulously creamy. The perfect coffee drink to enjoy on a hot summer day. This simple recipe is made in your very own kitchen. It only takes 5 minutes and 4 ingredients.

**Total Time: 5**

**Servings: 1**

| Ingredients | Directions |
|---|---|
| 1 Vanilla or Caramel Premier<br><br>Sugar free Caramel syrup<br><br>Shot of espresso<br><br>Ice | 1. Blend the premier protein shake, the sugar free syrup, espresso and Ice together until it reach the consistency of a frozen drink. |

# Raspberry delight

Fresh Raspberries, heavy cream and lemon zest are the stars in this awesome recipe! Blissfully sweet and tart, this creamy layered dessert could not be any dreamier.

**Total Time: 8 mint**

**Servings: 1**

## Ingredients

1 Vanilla premier shake

fresh raspberry

sugar free raspberry syrup

Mint

Lemon zest

Heavy cream

Ice

## Directions

1. Blend the premier shake, raspberry, sugar free raspberry syrup, and lemon juice together. Pour the mixer over ice, the Whip the heavy cream and lemon zest together. Place it on top of the raspberry mixer with mint leaf.

# Colorful Tuna

Healthy and refreshing flavors combine in this colorful, super simple tuna salad. Feel free to use any cooked protein in place of the tuna, if you like. It's the perfect light lunch!

**Total Time: 12 min**

**Servings:  2**

## Ingredients

3 pouches of lemon tuna

¼ c of Mayo

1T of Mustard

2 boiled eggs

¼ c of red bell peppers (diced)

¼ c of green bell peppers (diced)

¼ c of yellow bell peppers (diced)

1/4 c of Sweet Onions ( diced)

2 T Sweet relish

Salt

pepper

## Directions

1. Combine the tuna, chopped eggs, mayo, mustard, onions, sweet relish red, green & yellow bell peppers. Add salt and pepper to taste.

# Energy Bites

Looking for the best energy bites?

This 5 Ingredient peanut butter Energy Bites is loaded with old fashioned oats, peanut butter and flax seeds. A healthy protein packed breakfast or snack!

**Total Time: 50 min**

**Servings: 4**

| Ingredients | Directions |
|---|---|
| ½ c Peanut butter<br><br>1 ¼ c Rolled oat<br><br>1/3 c Honey<br><br>3 T Mini Chocolate chip<br><br>2 T Flax seeds<br><br>¼ tsp of kosher salt | 1. Place all ingredients in a large mixing bowl. Stir to combine. If the mixture feel a little to wet add a bit more oat or if feel a little to dry add a bit more honey or peanut butter. It should be somewhat sticky. Place it in the refrigerator for 30 minutes. Take a cookie scoop to make 1 inch balls.<br>2. Enjoy |

# Zucchini Noodles with Chicken Breast

This recipe is simple and absolutely satisfying – very light, low-carb and healthy recipe which quickly comes together!

**Total Time: 30 min**

**Servings: 2**

| Ingredients | Directions |
|---|---|

**Ingredients**

Zucchini noodles

¼ c White onions

2T Garlic

½ c Pesto sauce

Parmigiana Cheese

1 pound Chicken breast

Salt

Pepper

¼ c Extra Virgin Olive oil

1T Unsalted butter.

¼ c heavy cream

**Directions**

1. Season the chicken breast with extra virgin olive oil, salt and pepper. Grilled the breast until it reaches 165 degree. Let it stand for 3 to 5 minutes. Slice the chicken breast into chunks.
2. Place it to the side once it is done. Sauté onion and garlic until they are translucent.
3. Add your favorite pesto sauce and heavy cream to the pan then toss the zucchini noodles and chicken in the sauce. Sprinkle parmigiana cheese on top.

## Creamy Cajun Shrimp Pasta

This recipe makes for a meal that's easy to whip up and will become a part of your weeknight dinner rotation.

**Total Time: 30 mint**

**Servings: 4**

## Ingredients

kosher salt

1 lb. linguine

1 tbsp. exra-virgin olive oil

1 lb. large shrimp, peeled and deveined

Freshly ground black pepper

2 tbsp. Cajun seasoning

2 tbsp. butter

2 tbsp. all-purpose flour

3/4 c. heavy cream

1/2 c. freshly grated Parmesan, plus more for garnish

1/4 c. chopped

## Directions

1. Add salt to a pot of water and bring to a boil. Cook pasta to al dente. Take out ½ c of the pasta water then drain pasta and reserve 1 cup pasta water, and return to pot.
2. Meanwhile, in a large skillet over medium heat, heat olive oil.
3. Add shrimp and season with salt, pepper and Cajun seasoning. Cook until pink, 2 minutes per side, then transfer to a plate.
4. Wipe out skillet and add butter. Once melted, stir in flour and whisk until golden, 1 minute. Add heavy cream and whisk until creamy, then add Parmesan and 1/2 cup pasta water. Whisk until creamy, then season with salt and pepper.
5. Return pasta to skillet and toss until creamy, then add shrimp and parsley and toss until combined.
6. Garnish with Parmesan and

fresh parsley

serve.

# Conclusion

I want to appreciate and thank you for getting a copy of this cookbook. I hope and do believe you have gotten so much value from it. Always remember to stay away from junk food as they are detrimental to health and can seriously sabbotage your weight loss efforts. There are countless of tasty recipes you can make right from your home kitchen.

….Continue to stay healthy!

©**Chef Cynthia Monden**